Flower Drying
With A Microwave

Techniques and Projects

Flower Drying With A Microwave

Techniques and Projects

Titia Joosten

A Sterling/**Lark Book**

Sterling Publishing Co., Inc., New York

Published in 1989 by Sterling Publishing Co., Inc.,
387 Park Avenue South, New York, NY 10016.

A Sterling/Lark Book

Produced by Altamont Press, 50 College Street,
Asheville, North Carolina, 28801, U.S.A.

First published in the Netherlands under the title
Bloemen drogen in de magnetron een kwestie van minuten
Text © 1985 Titia Joosten-Franke
© 1985 Van Dishoeck/Unieboek bv, Weesp
English Edition © 1988 Altamont Press.

Translation: Marianne Weigman
Editing: Dawn Cusick
Photography: Studio Four Colour, Amsterdam and Studio
Veldkamp, Nijmegen
Plants: De Walburg Nursery
Drawings: Bronja Cramer
Typesetting: Diana Deakin
Assistance: Sandy Mush Herb Nursery

ISBN 0-937274-48-8

Every effort has been made to ensure that all information in this book
is accurate. However, due to differing conditions, microwave ovens,
and individual skills, the publisher cannot be responsible for any
injuries, losses, or other damage which may result from the use of the
information in this book.

Library of Congress Cataloging-in-Publication Data
Joosten, Titia.
  Flower drying with a Microwave.
  Translation of: Bloemen drogen in de magnetron, een kwestie van minuten.
  1. Flowers - Drying. 2. Plants - Drying. 3. Microwave ovens.
    4. Dried flower arrangement. I. Title
SB447.J6613 1988   745.92   88-80458
ISBN 0-937274-48-8

Front Cover photo:
An arrangement of Althaea rosea (hollyhock); Cornus florida var. rubra
(red flowering dogwood); Deutzia X rosea 'Carminea' (wedding bells);
Euphorbia myrsinites (myrtle Euphorbia); Hedera helix (ivy) preserved
with glycerin; Hydrangea 'Preziosa' (hydrangea); Majoraan origanum
vulgare (marjoram) with ivy wrapped in bunches; Rosa (lilac and pink
colored roses); Saxifraga umbrosa (leaf-rosette of London Pride).
Photo: Ed Suister

TABLE OF CONTENTS

INTRODUCTION

In many libraries and bookstores you'll find almost as many books about flower drying and arranging as there are varieties of flowers. The chapters on flower design and arrangement in these books are as personal and diverse as their authors, yet the chapters on methods to dry flowers are generally quite similar in content. This is because until now, there have been only a few flower drying methods to choose from: hanging, pressing, drying racks, and desiccants. Almost every description of these methods includes a warning that flower drying can't be rushed — beautiful results take time.

This is where my book differs from the rest. Between these pages I'll show you a marvelous new way to dry flowers and foliage in just a few minutes. House plants, trees, shrubs, bulb flowers, perennials, and annuals are preserved and ready for arranging in less time than it takes just to set up the materials for one of the traditional methods.

The book begins with a short review of the most common flower drying methods. The next section discusses the microwave oven. As common as microwaves are in everyday life, you may be tempted to skip this section. Don't! It's important to understand exactly how micro waves work to ensure good drying results.

It's also important to realize that, although your dried materials will be ready in minutes, designing and making bouquets is still a time-consuming process. No matter how fast the drying process, collecting a good inventory of color and variety still takes time. Not every flower blooms at the same time of year, and not every color is available in every locale. While you're working on developing this inventory, though, do liven up some of your old arrangements with freshly dried materials. You'll be amazed at the difference just a few additions can make.

A bouquet of dried flowers that you've designed and dried will give you pleasure every time you see it. Or give someone special this same pleasure with a beautiful yet inexpensive arrangement of flowers.

In all of your flower drying endeavors I wish you fun, success, and a small but much needed dose of patience.

Titia Joosten-Franke

CHAPTER ONE:
FLOWER DRYING PAST AND PRESENT

Archeologists have made very few discoveries of dried plants in ancient cultures, which is understandable when you consider how very fragile dried material is. When exposed to sunlight their colors fade, and in damp atmospheres flowers will often re-absorb moisture and wilt. Dried leaves, however, do not re-absorb moisture, making historical finds more likely. A head wreath of dried laurel leaves, for example, displayed at the British Museum in London, was found in a Roman grave in Egypt and dates back more than 2,000 years.

When scientists began collecting and classifying flower and plant species, they saved their work between the pages of books. These flowers and plants were never exposed to light or humidity, so their natural colors and shapes were preserved. One such scientific collection, called a herbarium, is more than 400 years old and still in good condition.

Drying by Pressing

The plant material scientists collected for their herbariums was dried between sheets of absorbent paper that were inserted between the pages of a thick book. In two to three weeks, the book's weight had pressed out the plant's moisture, which was absorbed by the paper. Although this drying method is still widely used

today, innovative flower dryers often experiment with different weights, such as bricks or boards, to press out the moisture.

Drying by Hanging

Flowers ideal for drying are called "everlastings." This group of flowers, mostly annuals, have papery or chaffy parts that retain their shape and color after being dried. The most common method of drying everlastings is by hanging, whch started in the middle ages. The flowers are tied together in small bunches and then hung upside down in a cool, dark place. Many herbs also dry well with this method. When it became fashionable in the 18th century to use dried flowers for decorative rather than symbolic purposes, the flowers were hung to dry and then made into bouquets that were preserved under glass.

Drying with Desiccants

Desiccants are moisture-absorbing substances, such as sand, silica gel, borax, and yellow cornmeal, that can be used to dry flowers. In the early 1600s, fresh flowers were dried between layers of sand. Although the sand method is still used today, many flower dryers have opted for silica gel because the silica granules weigh significantly less than sand granules and cause less flower damage. Flowers and plants dried in silica gel also tend to keep their shape and color better than with the sand method, which proves that faster drying times yield better results. (With silica gel, the drying process generally takes seven days, compared to two to three weeks with sand.)

Drying in the Microwave

The newest and fastest way to dry flowers is the microwave method. During the last few years I've experimented extensively with this method with astonishing results. The heat of the microwave evaporates the moisture in a flower or leaf, and this moisture is then absorbed by silica gel. After you've finished the chapter on microwaves you'll have a clearer understanding of how the whole process takes place.

———————

CHAPTER TWO:
WHAT IS SILICA GEL?

Technically, silica gel is a xerogel of silicic acid that has a strong absorbing property. Actually, it's not a gel at all, but a granular substance that closely resembles sugar. Each grain of silica gel can absorb up to 40% of its own weight in moisture, and for years it has been used commercially to protect moisture-sensitive products such as fine leathers and photographic materials. Silica gel is ideal for drying flowers because the small granules easily penetrate even the most delicate flower heads. Look for it in garden shops, drugstores, crafts shops, and floral shops.

In dry form, silica gel is blue, but the granules develop a whitish-pink color as they absorb moisture, so you can tell when silica granules have reached their saturation point by periodically checking their color. Silica gel can be re-used for years by removing the moisture from the granules each time they become saturated.

Always keep silica gel out of the reach of children. Although it's not toxic in itself, the granules will absorb the toxic insecticides of plants that have been sprayed. If you're one of those people who keeps their sugar in grandmother's old container marked "rice," protect yourself from an easy mistake by clearly labeling the silica gel and storing it outside of the kitchen. Silica gel tastes nothing like sugar or rice!

Drying Silica Gel For Re-Use

Always start by sifting through the silica gel to remove as much leftover plant material as possible.

Conventional Oven

Pre-heat the oven to 300° F (150° C). Spread a single layer of silica gel evenly on the bottom of a shallow pan and place it uncovered in the oven. Stir the granules every once in a while and watch for the return of their original blue color. When the granules are again blue, pour the silica in a pan with a tight-fitting cover and let cool. The pan and its cover should be pre-heated (either in the oven or with very hot water) to prevent condensation that would be absorbed by the silica gel. After cooling, immediately place the silica gel into a tight-fitting container to prevent the granules from absorbing any atmospheric moisture.

On the Stove

Spread the silica gel evenly in a low, wide frying pan. (Do not use the teflon-coated variety.) Heat the granules while stirring on medium heat until they become blue again. Cool and store them as described above.

In the Microwave

Do not dry more than 2 pounds (1 kilogram) at a time. Spread the granules in an open cardboard box or a microwavable dish. Place your container on a microwave drain rack so the moisture absorbed from the granules can escape from all sides of the container. Set the microwave at about 500 watts (medium high; setting #7; or on high if you have only high - low settings). In about ten minutes the granules will turn blue. Interrupt your cooking time every few minutes to stir the granules. Use the method above to cool and store the gel.

_____

_____

Warning: Silica gel often spreads fine dust particles that can irritate the mucus membranes. Avoid working in unventilated areas.

CHAPTER THREE:
UNDERSTANDING THE MICROWAVE

Forty years ago very few people had even heard of a micro wave, yet today more than half of all households use microwave ovens to save time and energy.

Scientists had known about micro waves for many years, but it wasn't until 1945 that a physicist accidently placed his lunch bag on a machine emitting very short radio waves (also called micro waves). When he removed his lunch, he discovered the bag's contents were thoroughly heated.

Microwave ovens differ from conventional ovens in the way heat is transferred to the food. In conventional ovens, the heat is transferred first to the pan or dish and then slowly moves to the food. In a microwave oven, the heat transfers directly to the food, not heating the containers at all.

What are Micro Waves

Micro waves — just like radio and television waves — are electromagnetic waves. These different waves distinguish themselves by the number of times they vibrate per second and by their length. Micro waves have a very high frequency and are very short. (The word "micro" comes from the Greek word *mikros*, meaning small.)

The Magnetron Tube

The most important part of the microwave oven is the magnetron tube. (In many countries microwave ovens are called magnetron ovens.) This tube works like a sending station and sends micro waves into the oven.

Dispersing the Micro Waves

The more evenly the magnetron disperses micro waves into the oven the better the cooking results. To disperse these waves evenly, the

Length of A Micro Wave

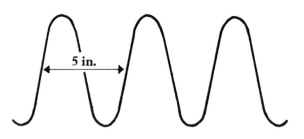

5 in.

microwave oven uses a bladed propeller that spins when the oven is started and spreads the waves in all directions. Some newer models use a turntable instead of a propeller to ensure even cooking.

How Micro Waves Work on Food and Flowers

To understand how micro waves work on food and flowers, it's important to know the following:

1. Micro waves penetrate only items that contain moisture.
2. Micro waves penetrate through porcelain, glass, plastic, cardboard, and paper the same way light penetrates through a window. These materials are neither heated nor affected by micro waves.

For example, when you prepare food in a glass dish or dry flowers in a cardboard box, you'll notice that the container remains cold while the contents become extremely hot. (Occasionally a container used in the microwave oven becomes heated, but this heat comes from the container's contents and *not* from micro waves.)

3. Micro waves bounce back from all metals the same way light reflects from a mirror. If you tried to cook food in a metal container in a microwave oven, the food would remain cold because the micro waves could not penetrate through to the food. (Never use anything metal in your microwave oven: it can cause serious damage to the oven's magnetron tube.)

How Micro Waves Create Heat

To cook or reheat food in a microwave oven, the food is usually placed in a covered dish without the addition of extra moisture or fat. When the oven is started, micro waves bounce back from the metal on the inside of the oven's walls and penetrate into the food in all directions about an inch (2½ - 3 cm.). Once these micro waves have penetrated the food, they quickly bring the food's naturally slow moving water molecules into a state of agitation. This agitation causes friction and the friction results in heat. (Heat results in a similar way when we rub our palms together: the faster we rub, the warmer our hands become.)

During this heating process the food's moisture evaporates. If left in the microwave too long, food will dry out. This drying-out effect, however, is exactly the result we're looking for when drying plants and flowers.

Microwave Oven Components

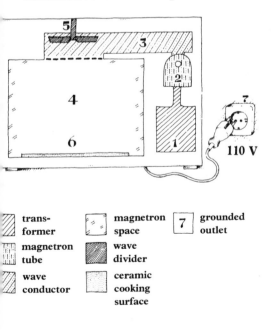

▨ transformer	▨ magnetron space	7 grounded outlet
▨ magnetron tube	▨ wave divider	
▨ wave conductor	▨ ceramic cooking surface	

How Fast Does Food Cook in a Microwave Oven?

The speed with which a microwave oven can heat food closely depends on the number of water molecules in that food. The more water molecules there are to be agitated, the longer it takes for heat to build up.

How Fast Do Flowers and Leaves Dry in a Microwave?

Flowers and leaves contain water molecules just as food does, and the quantity of these molecules varies from flower to flower, just as the quantity of water molecules varies from vegetable to vegetable.

The number of flowers or leaves you're drying at one time also determines the drying time. Two roses have twice as many water molecules as one rose; consequently the drying time is twice as long. (Drying times do not always increase proportionately with the number of items, however.)

Are all Microwave Ovens the Same?

Obviously, all microwave ovens are not the same. (A quick glance at the price tags can confirm this!) The more expensive ovens have a larger cooking capacity, averaging 1,000 to 1,400 watts. About half of this wattage is used to produce micro waves, leaving 500 to 700 watts left to actually heat the food.

Cheaper models generally have less wattage available to heat food, and take more time to cook the same item.

Microwaves also vary in their number of settings, ranging from choices of two settings (high and low/defrost) to four settings, all the way up to ten settings on some expensive models. For drying flowers and leaves, the best results are achieved by using the oven's lower settings.

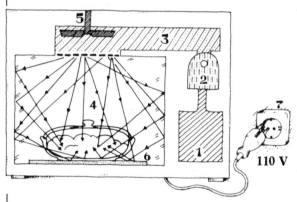

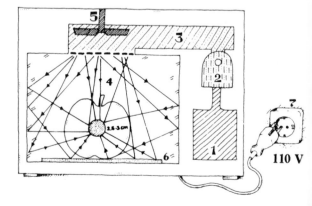

Above, micro waves penetrate through the glass and into the food.

Right, micro waves bounce back on the metal inside the oven.

Are Microwave Ovens Dangerous?

Occasionally we still hear rumors that cooking with microwave ovens is dangerous. People who believe this obviously do not understand that micro waves belong to the family of non-ionized electromagnetic waves. Or maybe people worry that the oven could work as well on human skin as it does on food. If microwave ovens could work with the door open, this would be a legitimate concern. But international safety codes require all microwaves to build several switches into the oven's door that cut off the oven's power when the door is opened. Since these switches work independently of each other, you're still protected even if one switch breaks.

Energy Savings

On the average, microwave ovens use 35% less energy to cook the same food as conventional ovens and burners. On low settings the energy savings are proportionally less.

The Fun Begins

Now that you're familiar with how the microwave oven works and with all the jargon, you're ready to start using the microwave to quickly dry flowers for your own bouquets and wreaths.

CHAPTER FOUR:
MATERIALS AND TOOLS

To dry flowers and leaves in the microwave you'll need:

- ☐ floral scissors
- ☐ tweezers
- ☐ 5 to 7 pounds (2 to 3 kilograms) of fine-grained silica gel
- ☐ large spoon
- ☐ wooden toothpicks
- ☐ fine paintbrush (for removing granules from delicate flower heads)
- ☐ cardboard boxes to store unused dried material
- ☐ microwavable dishes or cardboard boxes, preferably with a tight-fitting top. (Before using cardboard boxes, be sure to check for and remove any metal staples that could damage your microwave.)
- ☐ a microwave thermometer is also a worthwhile investment. Meat thermometers with a scale from 130 to 195° F (55 to 90°) can also be used, but because they contain metal they can only be used after the microwave is turned off.

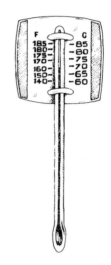

This microwave thermometer contains no mercury and will not damage a microwave oven.

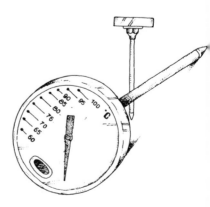

Because it contains metal, this meat thermometer can only be used after the microwave oven is turned off.

CHAPTER FIVE:
FLOWERS SUITABLE FOR DRYING

The pleasures of flower drying begin when you gather your fresh materials. What a wealth of wildflowers, grasses, and cultivated flowers the world contains! Even in the smallest yard there's something to be found. City dwellers will be surprised at the variety available from florists. Flowers that were until recently found only in private gardens are now being sold in small bunches ideal for drying.

In principle all flowers can be dried, although with every method the colors usually dry a little lighter or darker. Generally, the most vividly colored flowers are the most colorfast. It's also not necessary that your dried flowers look exactly like their fresh counterparts. A good dried arrangement combines flowers from different bloom seasons, and it's just this ability to use out-of-bloom flowers and leaves that makes dried flower arrangements so special.

Flowers with thick petals — such as Clematis vitelba, Hyacinth, Iris, and Magnolia — do not dry well even in the microwave. In Chapter 9 you'll find a list of flowers I've tested and how to dry them.

No doubt you'll encounter varieties in your own garden and in local flower shops that I haven't tested, and to dry them you'll have to do some experimenting. To start, look through the flower list for a flower similar to yours and try drying it using those instructions. You may not get perfect results the first time, but even your test flowers can be used later to fill in the base of a bouquet. Be sure to record your drying times and temperatures in the chart in Chapter 10 for future reference.

Choose a flower with simple structure — such as a marigold — for your first time drying in the microwave. Be sure to pick your flowers just before their height in flowering. (Flowers picked in full bloom lose their petals during drying.)

Generally, flower buds cannot be dried because the silica gel can't penetrate through to the bud's center. Some small buds, though, such as Exochorda (pearlbush) and Geum (avens) can be dried.

Avoid picking flowers when they're wet from rain or dew. (If you come across some wet flowers you just can't resist, let them stand in a vase until the petals are dry before microwaving.)

Leaves are usually dried separately from flowers because their drying times are so much shorter.

CHAPTER SIX:
LEAVES SUITABLE FOR DRYING

Without greenery, an arrangement of dried flowers is never complete. Greenery serves as a calming backdrop to the wonderful colors and soft curves of dried flowers. For some reason, commercially-made arrangements usually lack enough greenery, and consequently are inferior to those made at home. If there's a commercially-made dried flower arrangement in your home or office that you pass by daily without noticing, add a few dried branches to give it new life. You'll immediately notice the colors seem more vivid and the arrangement looks more natural. For this reason alone it is well worth your time to build up a good supply of dried leaves.

Drying leaves in the microwave opens up a new realm of possibilities because leaves that are almost impossible to dry using other methods will dry well in a microwave. For instance, the fleshy stems of the Euphorbia Mysinites (Myrtle Euphorbia) and the leathery leaf rosettes of Saxifraga Umbrosa (London Pride) dry easily in the microwave. Both of these leaves become an olive green after drying and are shown in the cover arrangement. (If you pick these leaf rosettes late in the summer, they'll have the shape of a flat flower.)

For the best results, always dry leaves that are full grown and look for as much variation in color and shape as possible. If you're drying a leaf variety not mentioned in Chapter 12, look through the list to find a leaf similar to your choice and use those directions as a starting point for your own experimentation. Once you've achieved satisfactory results, record your method in Chapter 13.

CHAPTER SEVEN:
DRYING IN THE MICROWAVE OVEN

Preparing your plant material

Gather all of your materials together before starting. Different varieties of flowers and leaves should never be dried together because each flower has its own unique drying time.

Most flowers will hold their shape better if dried in an upright position, although branches with multiple blossoms should be dried lying flat. When drying in the upright position, cut the stem off about 1¼ inches (3 cm) from the flower. (Floral wire is later attached to this piece of stem.) For flowers with thin, fragile stems, a wooden toothpick is stuck through the bottom of the flower (next to or through the stem). When the flower is dried, the floral wire can be attached to the toothpick or the pick can be removed and the wire threaded through the hole.

With double flowers, such as tea roses, the petals folded over one another must be removed prior to drying. (Tweezers work well for this.) You may be upset at removing such beautiful petals, but for the drying process to work the silica gel has to penetrate the flower's head.

All leaves (with the exception of leaf rosettes, such as Pachysandra) are dried lying flat.

To start the drying process, layer 1¼ inches (3 cm) of silica gel on the bottom of your container with a spoon. Place the flowers or leaves on top of this layer, leaving 1¼ inches (3 cm) between the container's sides and between individual flowers. Sprinkle silica gel around the plant's edges, and then add another 1¼ inch (3 cm) layer of silica gel on top.

Place your uncovered container in the microwave. If you're using a cardboard box, elevate it on a microwavable drain rack so the moisture can escape through the bottom of the box.

Silica gel granules are sprinkled carefully over flowers.

What Setting to Use

If your microwave has settings from 2 to 10, put it on setting #4 (about 300 watts); a microwave with 3 or 4 settings should be put on "half" (about 350 watts); and a microwave with a "high" and "defrost" setting should be put on "defrost" (about 200 watts).

Microwave Drying Times

Because there's so much variation in microwaves and in the amount of moisture a particular plant contains, it's impossible to predict exactly how long the cooking time should be. The number of items you're drying and the amount of moisture in your silica gel will also affect the cooking time. Roughly, the drying time for one or more flowers/leaves in about ½ pound (300 kg) of silica gel is 2 to 2½ minutes; in about 2¼ pounds (1 kg) of silica gel, 5 to 6 minutes; and in about 3½ pounds (1½ kg) silica gel, 6 to 7 minutes.

Using a Thermometer or Thermo-Needle

For more exact work you can use a thermometer or a thermo-needle to determine the temperature of the silica gel. With this method you don't have to be concerned about how many kilowatts your microwave has or how long to set the timer.

If you're using a microwavable (non-metal) thermometer, just stick it down between the flowers in the silica gel in a way that you can read the temperature through the microwave door. Stop cooking when the silica gel reaches the required temperature. (Chapters 9 and 12 indicate the temperatures the silica gel has to reach for each flower and leaf.) Obviously, the more plant material you're drying at one time, the longer it will take to reach the required temperature.

When using a meat thermometer (or other metal thermometer), set the timer for short periods of time and measure the silica gel's temperature *outside* your oven to prevent damage to your magnetron tube. If the necessary temperature is still not reached, then remove the thermometer and cook again for another short period of time.

Standing Time

Most people who use microwave ovens know that foods cooked in a microwave contain so much heat that they continue cooking even after the oven is shut off and need standing time. Flowers and leaves dried in the microwave also need standing time. For fragile flowers with only a few petals, the time is usually about 10 minutes. For sturdy, full flowers the standing time can range up to 30 minutes. To prevent moisture from forming (and being re-absorbed by your flowers), put a lid on your container and leave it cracked just a bit.

When the standing time has finished, empty the box or dish onto a newspaper and gently remove the flowers. If the flowers are sturdy, you can remove the silica gel by shaking them; if they're fragile, use a fine paintbrush. (If some of the granules continue to stick, store the flowers in a tightly-closed box and they'll eventually fall off.)

Inspect the stems and flower centers to be sure they're completely dry; if not, cover only the damp parts with silica gel and microwave them again for a short time on the same setting you used before. Allow the silica gel to cool in between batches of flowers.

A paintbrush removes silica granules on delicate flowers.

Cleaning the Microwave

On your oven's highest setting, bring a cup of water with a dash of lemon juice to a boil. Change the temperature setting to "low" and boil for 3 minutes. Then thoroughly dry the inside of the microwave and its door. Your oven will be shining clean and the kitchen will smell fresh!

CHAPTER EIGHT:
SPECIAL FLOWERS, SPECIAL CARE

Although drying flowers with the microwave and silica gel is the preferred method, some flowers dry better using just silica gel. Passiflora (passionflower), Lilac, Viburnum, and the bracts of Cornus (dogwood), for example, dry to a fried brown in the microwave, yet retain their color when dried in silica gel alone. With other flowers, such as Freesias and Dahlias, the silica granules are difficult to remove without damaging the flower when dried in the microwave, and should also be dried in silica gel alone.

For delicate flowers that need wire stems, silica gel often works better because the flowers can be wired *before* drying. (Flowers dried in the microwave have to be wired *after* they're dried, when they're more likely to shatter.)

CHAPTER NINE:
TESTED FLOWERS FROM A TO Z

Flowers described as "moistureproof" tend not to re-absorb moisture after they've been dried and can better tolerate moist environments. If you're starting with a plant's common name, you can find its Latin name in the alphabetized list on pages 68 - 71. The temperature column indicates the temperature the silica gel must reach before removing your flowers from the microwave.

Latin Name (Common Name)		Temp.	Remarks
Acacia decurrens (mimosa)		160 F 70 C	Moistureproof; leaves can be dried at the same time as the flowers; can also be dried by hanging.
Achillaea millefolium (yarrow)		160 F 70 C	Moistureproof.
Althea rosea (hollyhock)	single	150 F 65 C	
	double	160 F 70 C	
Anemone coronaria (windflower or poppy anemone)	single	140 F 60 C	The vividly colored flowers will fade slightly.
	double	150 F 65 C	
Anethum graveolens (dill)		150 F 65 C	Moistureproof.
Anthemis nobilis (common chamomile)		160 F 70 C	Moistureproof.
Anthemis tinctoria (golden marguerite or chamomile)		160 F 70 C	Moistureproof.
Aquilegia hybrid (columbine)		160 F 70 C	

Latin Name (Common Name)	Temp.	Remarks
Asclepias tuberosa (butterfly weed)	160 F 70 C	Moistureproof.
Astilbe chinensis 'Pumila' (dwarf goat's beard)	170 F 75 C	Moistureproof.
Astilbe hybrid (astilbe)	160 F 70 C	Moistureproof.
Astrantia	160 F 70 C	Moistureproof.
Astrantia helleborefolia	160 F 70 C	Moistureproof.
Astrantia major (masterwort)	160 F 70 C	Moistureproof.
Astrantia major rosea	160 F 70 C	Moistureproof.
Aubrietia deltoidea (rockcress)	150 F 65 C	Cluster several flowerettes together and secure with floral wire before using in bouquets.
Bouvardia	150 F 65 C	The white flowers become grey after microwaving.
Buphthalmum salicifolium (golden beauty)	160 F 70 C	
Caltha palustris (cowslip, marsh marigold)	150 F 65 C	Moistureproof.
Caryopteris clandonensis (ferndown, bluebeard)	150 F 65 C	
Centaurea montana (bachelor button)	150 F 65 C	Moistureproof.
Chrysanthenum carinatum (painted daisy, annual)	150 F 65 C	
Chrysanthenum parthenium (feverfew)	160 F 70 C	Moistureproof.
Chrysanthenum segetum	170 F 75 C	Moistureproof.
Corylopsis pauciflora (winter hazel)	160 F 70 C	
Cosmos bipinnatus (cosmos)	150 F 65 C	

Latin Name (Common Name)	Temp.	Remarks
Cosmos sulphureus 'Sunset' (orange, yellow cosmos)	160 F 70 C	
Crambe cordifolia (colewort)	170 F 75 C	Moistureproof.
Cystisus praecox (warminster broom)	160 F 70 C	Moistureproof.
Cystisus scoparius (Scotch broom)	160 F 70 C	Moistureproof.
Dahlia		Moistureproof; silica granules tend to stick to the petals when dried in the microwave; better to choose another method.
Delphinium ajacis (annual larkspur)	170 F 75 C	Moistureproof.
Delphenium hybrid (delphinium)	170 F 75 C	Slightly less moistureproof than the annual larkspur; the white flowers turn light blue after microwaving.
Deutzia hybrid X ('Magician')	150 F 65 C	Moistureproof; the leaves can be dried at the same time as the flowers.
Deutzia X kalmiiflora	160 F 70 C	" "
Deutzia X rosea 'Carminea'	160 F 70 C	" "
Deutzia scabra (weddingbells)	150 F 65 C	" "
Digitalis purpurea (foxglove)	170 F 75 C	Remove closed buds before drying; the pink flowers retain their color the best.
Dimorphotheca sinuata (cape marigold)	150 F 65 C	
Epimedium alpinum and E. versicolor 'Sulhureum' (bishop's head)	150 F 65 C	Moistureproof; cluster several flowerettes together and secure with floral wire before using in bouquets.
Erica gracilis (heath)	150 F 65 C	Moistureproof.
Erica versicolor var. costata	160 F 70 C	Moistureproof.

Latin Name (Common Name)	Temp.	Remarks
Eryngium alpine 'Donard'	175 F 80 C	Moistureproof.
Escallonia	160 F 70 C	Moistureproof; the branches can be dried at the same time as the flowers and leaves; leaves dry to an olive green color.
Eschscholzia (California poppy)	140 F 60 C	Very fragile after drying; can also be dried by hanging.
Eupatorium purpureum (purple Joe-Pye-weed)	170 F 75 C	Moistureproof; dry when still in bud.
Euphorbia fulgens (scarlet plume spurge)	160 F 70 C	Moistureproof.
Exochorda giraldii (pearlbush)	150 F 65 C	Moistureproof; branches can be dried with flowers and leaves.
Freesia		The silica granules tend to stick to the petals when dried in the microwave; better to choose another method.
Fuchsia	170 F 75 C	
Gaura	160 F 70 C	Moistureproof.
Gazania splendens (treasure flower)	150 F 65 C	
Geranium macrorrhizum (form of Cranesbill)	150 F 65 C	
Gerbera (African daisy)	160 F 70 C	The flowers must be very fresh when they're dried or the petals will fall off.
Geum hybrid (avens)	150 F 65 C	
Geum rivale (purple avens)	150 F 65 C	
Hamamelis 'Feuerzauber' (witch hazel)	160 F 70 C	Moistureproof.
Hamamelis mollis (Chinese witch hazel)	160 F 70 C	Moistureproof.
Hemerocallis (day lily)	160 F 70 C	Handle the dried flowers carefully, they're very fragile.

Latin Name (Common Name)	Temp.	Remarks
Heracleum (cow parsnip)	160 F 70 C	Moistureproof; dry only the loose flowers.
Hesperus matronalis	160 F 70 C	
Heuchera sanguinea (coral bells)	160 F 70 C	Moistureproof.
Hoya carnosa (waxflower)	175 F 80 C	Moistureproof.
Hydrangea macrophylla (big leaf hydrangea)	160 F 70 C	Moistureproof; dry during different bloom cycles; the branches are beautiful in bouquets.
Hydrangea paniculata (hydrangea)	170 F 75 C	Moistureproof.
Hydrangea petiolaris (climbing hydrangea)	175 F 80 C	Moistureproof; dry the flowers when the middle flowerettes are still partially in buds.
Hypericum (St. John's wort)	150 F 65 C	
Iberis sempervirens (evergreen candytuft)	150 F 65 C	Moistureproof.
Kalanchoe	175 F 80 C	
Kerria japonica (Japanese kerria) single	150 F 65 C	Moistureproof.
double	170 F 75 C	
Limnanthes douglasii (poached egg flower)	150 F 65 C	Cluster several flowers together and secure with floral wire before using in bouquets.
Lisianthus	150 F 65 C	
Lunaria biennis (honesty, moneyplant)	150 F 65 C	Chapter 15 explains how to dry the silicles.
Lupinus hartwegii (annual lupine)	160 F 70 C	Moistureproof.
Lupinus polyphyllus (form of lupine)	170 F 75 C	Moistureproof; remove the tip of the flower before drying.

Latin Name (Common Name)	Temp.	Remarks
Lysimachia clethroides (gooseneck)	170 F 75 C	Moistureproof.
Meconopsis betonicifolia (blue poppy)	150 F 65 C	The dried flower is somewhat fragile.
Myosotis alpestris (forget-me-not)	150 F 65 C	Moistureproof; bind the dried flowers together in a bunch prior to using.
Narcissus (daffodil)	160 F 70 C	
Ornithogalum umbellatum (star of Bethlehem)	150 F 65 C	
Ornithogalum nutans	150 F 65 C	
Passiflora coerulea (passionflower)		The flowers turn brown when dried in the microwave; dry them instead in silica gel for 5 to 7 days.
Philadelphus coronarius (mock orange)	150 F 65 C	Dry branches with flowers and leaves.
Philadelphus 'Bouquet Blanc' (double mock orange)	160 F 70 C	
Phyllodoce erectus	160 F 70 C	Moistureproof.
Polemonium foliosissimum (Jacob's ladder)	160 F 70 C	
Polygonum affine (fleece flower)	170 F 75 C	Moistureproof.
Polygonum bistorta (pink knot weed)	175 F 80 C	Moistureproof.
Polygonum campanulata	150 F 65 C	Moistureproof.
Polygonum cuspidatum (Mexican bamboo)	150 F 65 C	Moistureproof; the leaves can be dried at the same time as the flowers.
Ranunculus (buttercup or crowfoot) single	160 F 70 C	Remove flower petals folded over each other with tweezers before
double	170 F 75 C	drying.

Latin Name (Common Name)	Temp.	Remarks
Robinia pseudoacacia (black locust)	160 F 70 C	
Rosa (such as tea rose)	170 F 75 C	Moistureproof; remove flower petals folded over each other with
single kind	160 F 70 C	tweezers before drying.
Rudbeckia purpurea 'The King' (purple coneflower)	170 F 75 C	Moistureproof; dry only very fresh flowers or they'll turn brown after microwaving.
Saxifraga (rockfoil)	150 F 65 C	Moistureproof; cluster several flowerettes together and secure with floral wire before using in bouquets.
Scabiosa atropurpurea plena (pin cushion flower) single	140 F 60 C	
double	150 F 65 C	
Scabiosa caucasia (pin cushion flower)	140 F 60 C	
Sedum spectabile (showy sedum)	175 F 80 C	Moistureproof; the flowers dry to a purple/brown and the buds to a bronze/green.
Smilacina racemosa (false Solomon's seal)	170 F 75 C	Moistureproof.
Solidago canadensis (goldenrod)	160 F 70 C	Moistureproof.
Solidaster luteus	150 F 65 C	Moistureproof; the leaves can be dried at the same time as the flowers.
Spiraea arguta (foam of May)	140 F 60 C	Moistureproof; the leaves and branches can be dried at the same time as the flowers.
Spiraea vanhoutii (Vanhoutte spirea)	140 F 60 C	" "
Syringa (lilacs)		Becomes brown in microwave; dry in silica gel for 4 - 5 days.
Tagetes (marigold)	170 F 75 C	
Tiarella polyphylla and T. wherryi (foamflower)	140 F 60 C	Moistureproof.

Latin Name (Common Name)	Temp.	Remarks
Trollius (globeflower)	150 F 65 C	Very poisonous.
Tulipa (tulip)	150 F 65 C	Store dried tulips in egg cartons until usage to prevent damage.
Veronica (speedwell)	170 F 75 C	Moistureproof.
Viburnum X bodnantense 'Dawn' (snowball)		Moistureproof; Viburnum becomes brown when dried in microwave; dry them instead in silica gel for 5 to 7 days.
Viburnum opulus (Guelder rose)	"	"
Viburnum opulus 'Sterile'	"	"
Viburnum tomentosum 'Mariesii' (double viburnum)	"	"
Viola (pansy)	150 F 65 C	
Zinnia elegans	170 F 75 C	Moistureproof.

CHAPTER TEN:
PERSONAL NOTES ON FLOWER DRYING

Latin Name	Common Name	Silica Gel Temperature	Remarks

Opposite Page:

Altaea rosea (hollyhock); Anemone coronaria (windflower); Astrantia major alba maxima (white masterwort); Astrantia major rosea; Cosmos; Deutzia X rosea 'Carminea'; Fagus (beech leaf preserved with glycerine); Hydrangea macrophylla (big leaf hydrangea); Leycesteria formosa, leaves with berries; Lysimachia clethroides (gooseneck); Polygonum affine (fleece flower); Rosa (rose); Saxifraga umbrosa (Leaf rosette of saxifraga); Tulipa (tulip); Viburnum opulus 'Sterile' (smowball); Zinnia elegans.

Page 34:

Anemone coronaria (anemone); Cornus kousa var. chinensis (form of dogwood); Delphinium ajacis (larkspur); Hydrangea (hydrangea), Pachysandra terminalis; Scabiosa caucasica (pin cushion flower); Fern.

Page 35:

Astrantia major (masterwort); Astrantia major alba maxima (white masterwort); Astantia maxima helleborefolia; Fagus (beech leaf preserved with glycerine); Leycesteria formosa, leaves with berries; Lysimachia clethroides (gooseneck), Nigella damascena (seedpods of love-in-a-mist); Zinnia elegans.

Page 36, top:

Achillae (yarrow); Asiatum tenerum 'Farleyense' (maidenhair fern); Carthamus tintorius (distaff thistle); Dahlia; Euphorbia fulgens; Hamamelis mollis (witch hazel); Hemerocallis (day lily); Narcissus (daffodil); Ponpondahlia (pompondahlia); Zinnia elegans.

Page 36, bottom:

Adiantum tenerum 'Farleyense' (maidenhair fern); Amaranthus caudatus 'Virides' (love-lies-bleeding); Anemone coronaria (anemone); Astrantia major rosea (masterwort); Astrantia maxima helleborefolia; Bouvardia; Deutzia scabra (wedding bells); Digitalis purpurea (foxglove); Eucalyptus-leaf; Exochorda giraldii; Freesia; Fuchsia; Gerbera, Geum; Lupinus polyphyllus (lupine); Lysimachia clethroides (gooseneck); Nigella damascena (seedpods of love-in-a-mist); Philadelphus coronarius (mock orange); Phyllothamnus erectus (ericaceae, heath); Polygonum bistorta (pink fleece flower); Rudbeckia purpurea 'The King' (purple coneflower); Tulipa (red and white tulips); fern leaves.

Page 38

Achillea millefolium 'Fire King' (yarrow); Cornus florida var. rubra (Florida dogwood); Dahlia; Tulipa (tulip); Syringa (lilac).

Astilbe 'Hyacinth';
Astrantia major (masterwort);
Astrantia helleborefolia;
Astrantia 'Shaggy'; Hydrangea paniculata (hydrangea);
Rosa (rose);
Epimedium en Fagus (Bishop's hat).

Alchemilla mollis;
Asclepias tuberosa (butterfly weed);
Caltha palustris (marsh marigold);
Deutzia X kalmiiflora;
Exochorda giraldii (pearlbush);
Geum (avens);
Limnanthes douglasii (poached egg flower);
Physalis alkekengi 'Franchettii';
Eucalyptus porriniana.

Anemone coronaria (windflower or poppy anemone);
Corylopsis pauciflora (winter hazel);
Deutzia scabra (wedding bells);
Euphorbia griffithii 'Fireglow';
Myosotis alpestris (forget-me-not);
Scabiosa caucasica (pin cushion flower);
Carpinifolia 'Wredei'.

Latin Name	Common Name	Silica Gel Temperature	Remarks

CHAPTER ELEVEN:
FLOWER NAMES BY COLOR

The list below may help if you're looking for dried flowers of a certain color. The flowers either retain their original color or change to the color listed.

White

Centaurea Montana .... bachelor's button
Chrysanthenum parthenium .... fever few
Cosmos
Crambe cordifolia .... colewort
Dahlia
Deutzia X kalmiiflora and Deutzia scabra
Exochorda giraldii .... pearlbush
Freesia
Gaura
Helleborus niger .... Christmas rose
Heracleum .... cow parsnip
Hoya carnosa (white with pink) .... waxflower
Hydrangea macrophylla .... French hydrangea
Hydrangea paniculata .... hydrangea
Hydrangea petiolaris .... climbing hydrangea
Iberis sempervirens .... evergreen candytuft
Lisianthus
Lunaria biennis .... honesty, money plant
Lysimachia cletroides .... gooseneck
Myosotis alpestris .... forget-me-not
Narcissus .... daffodil
Ornithogalum nutans (green-white)
Ornithogalum umbellatum .... star of Bethlehem
Passiflora coerulea (blue-white) .... passionflower
Polemonium caeruleum .... Greek valerian
Saxifrage .... rockfoil
Spiraea arguta .... bridal wreath, foam of May
Syringa .... lilac
Tulipa .... tulip
Viburnum opulus (pink-white) .... Guelder rose
Viburnum opulus 'Sterile' .... snowball
Viburnum tomentosum 'Mariesii' .... double file

Beige - White

Anemone coronaria .... wind flower
Astilbe 'Deutschland'
Astrantia major (white-red) .... masterwort
Astrantia major alba maxima (white-red) .... masterwort
Delphinium ajacis .... annual larkspur
Delphinium X cultorum .... larkspur
Digitalis purpurea 'Alba' .... foxglove
Erica gracilis .... heath
Euphorbia fulgens .... scarlet plume spurge
Freesia
Gerbera .... transvaal daisy
Lupinus hartwegii
Lupinus polyphyllus
Philadelphus coronarius .... mock orange
Philadelphus 'Bouquet Blanc' .... double mock orange
Robinia pseudoacacia .... black locust
Rosa .... rose
Scabiosa atropurpurea plena .... pin cushion flower
Smilacina racemosa .... false Solomon seal
Spiraea vanhouttii .... bridal wreath
Tiarella polyphylla and T. wherryi .... foam flower
Zinnia elegans

Grey

White Bouvardia

Yellow

Acacia decurrens .... mimosa
Althea Rosea .... hollyhock
Anethenum graveolens .... dill
Anthemis tinctoria
Buphthalmum salicifolium .... golden beauty
Caltha palustris .... marsh marigold
Chrysanthenum carinatum .... painted daisy
Corylopsis pauciflora
Cytisus praecox .... warminster broom
Cytisus scoparius .... Scotch broom
Dahlia
Dimorphotheca .... African daisy
Epimedium versicolor 'Sulphureum' .... bishop's head

Eschscholzia .... California popp

Euphorbia fulgens .... spurg

Freesia

Gerbera

Geum

Hamamelis mollis .... Chinese witch haz

Hemerocallis .... dayli

Hypernicum .... St. John's wo

Kalanchoe

Kerria japonica .... Japanese kerri

Limnanthes douglasii (yellow-white) .... poached egg flowe

Narcissus .... daffod

Ranunculus .... buttercu

Solidago canadensis .... goldenro

Solidaster luteus

Tagetes .... marigol

Tulipa .... tuli

Viola .... pans

Zinnia elegans

Pink

Achillea millefolium .... yarro

Althea rosea .... hollyhoc

Anemone coronaria .... wind flowe

Aquilegia hybrid .... columbin

Astilbe chinensis pumila .... dwarf goat's bear

Astilbe 'Hyacinth'

Astrantia major rosea .... masterwor

Astrantia maxima helleborefolia

Aubrieta deltoidea .... rockcres

Bouvardia

Centaurea montana .... bachelor's butto

Cosmos

Dahlia

Delphinium ajacis .... larkspu

Delphinium ruysii 'Pink Sensation'

Digitalis purpurea .... foxglov

Erica gracilis .... heat

Erica versicolor var. costata (pink-red)

Freesia (dark-pink and salmon-pink)

Fuchsia

Geranium macrorrhizum (blush-pink, pink-red buds) .... cranesbi

Gerbera

Hydrangea macrophylla .... big leaf hydrange

Kalanchoe

Pink (continued)

Lisianthus (blush-pink)
Lupinus hartwegii .... annual lupine
Lupinus polyphillus .... lupine
Myosotis alpestris .... forget-me-not
Polygonum affine .... fleece flower
Polygonum affine 'Superbum' (pink-red) .... pink fleece flower
Polygonum bistorta .... pink knot weed
Polygonum campanulatum .... knot weed
Polygnum cuspidatum (dark-pink) .... Mexican bamboo
Rosa .... rose
Rudbeckia purpurea 'The King' (pink-red) .... corn flower
Scabiosa atropurpurea plena .... pin cushion flower
Tulipa .... tulip
Zinnia elegans

Red

Dahlia
Euphorbia fulgens .... scarlet plume spurge
Freesia (red-brown)
Gerbera (red-brown) .... transvaal daisy
Heuchera sanguinea .... coral bells
Kalanchoe
Rosa .... rose
Tulipa .... tulip

Purple

Althea rosea (shining purple) .... hollyhock
Anemone coronaria .... wind flower
Aquilegia hybrid .... columbine
Aubrieta deltoidea .... rockcress
Chrysanthenum carinatum .... painted daisy
Cosmos
Delphinium hybrid .... blue larkspur
Erica gracilis .... heath
Escallonia (purple-white)
Eupatorium purpureum .... Joe-Pye-weed
Fuchsia
Helleborus orientalis (light-purple) .... Christmas rose
Lisianthus
Scabiosa atropurpurea plena .... pin cushion flower
Sedum spectabile (purple-brown) .... showy sedum
Syringa .... lilac
Tulipa (purple-black) .... tulip
Viola .... pansy

Burgundy

Achillea millefolium .... yarr
Aquilegia hybrid .... columbi
Astilbe 'Fanal' and 'Bremen'
Bouvardia
Chrysanthemum carinatum .... painted dai
Dahlia
Epimedium alpinum .... bishop's he
Eschscholzia .... California pop
Fuchsia
Gerbera .... transvaal dai
Lupinus hartwegii .... annual lupi
Lupinus polyphyllus .... lupi
Scabiosa atropurpurea plena
Tulipa .... tu
Zinnia elegans

Orange

Asclepias tuberosa .... butterfly we
Cosmos sulphureus 'Sunset'
Dimorphotheca .... cape marigo
Eschscholzia .... California pop
Euphorbia fulgens .... scarlet plume supr
Freesia (pale-orange)
Gerbera .... transvaal dai
Geum .... ave
Hamamelis 'Feuerzauber' (orange-brown) .... witch haz
Tagetes .... marigo
Zinnia elegans

Lilac

Aubrietia deltoidea .... rockcre
Cosmos
Deutzia 'Magician' (lilac-white)
Deutzia rosea 'Carminea'
Digitalis purpurea .... foxglo
Lunaria biennis (lilac-purple) .... money pla
Lupinus hartegii .... annual lupi
Lupinus polyphyllus .... Russell lupi
Rose 'Sterling Silver'
Syringa (lilac-purple) lil
Tulipa .... tul
Zinnia elegans

Light Blue

Delphinium ajacis .... annual larkspur
Delphinium hybrid .... delphinium
Myosotis alpestris .... forget-me-not
Polemonium caeruleum
Scabiosa atropurpurea plena (light lavender-blue) .... pin cushion flower
Scabiosa caucasica (light lavender-blue)
Viola .... pansy

Blue

Anemone coronaria .... wind flower
Aubrieta deltoidea .... rockcress
Caryopteris clandonensis .... ferndown, blue beard
Centaurea montana .... bachelor's button
Delphinium ajacis .... annual larkspur

CHAPTER TWELVE:
TESTED LEAVES FROM A TO Z

All leaves listed below are moistureproof. Also included in the list are bract that are worth drying.

Latin Name (Common Name)	Temp.	Remarks
Acanthus mollis (bear's breeches) leaves	140 F 60 C	The leaves dry to a bronze/green; the bract tips dry to a bronze colo
bracts	170 F 75 C	
Acacia decurrens (mimosa)	160 F 70 C	
Acer (maple)	140 F 60 C	Pick Acer leaves for drying during different seasons for dramatic colc differences.
Adiantum brisanthus (large maidenhair fern)	170 F 75 C	Can only be dried in the microwave.
Adiantum monocolar (small maidenhair fern)	150 F 65 C	
Adiantum tenerum 'Farleyense' (medium maidenhair fern)	150 F 65 C	
Althaea rosea (hollyhock)	150 F 65 C	
Aquilegia hybrid (columbine)	150 F 65 C	
Artemisia ludoviciana 'Silver Queen' (wormwood)	170 F 75 C	
Artemisia	170 F 75 C	
Astilbe hybrid	160 F 70 C	
Astrantia (masterwort)	150 F 65 C	

Latin Name (Common Name)	Temp.	Remarks
Ballota pseudodictamnus	150 F 65 C	
Beloperone guttata (shrimp-plant)	150 F 65 C	Beloperone is dried because of the beige/green or brown/pink bracts.
Bergenia cordifolia (bergenia)	160 F 70 C	Can only be dried in the microwave; the leaves dry to an olive green.
Blechnum spicant (deer fern)	150 F 65 C	
Bougainvillea glabra (paper flower)	140 F 60 C	Bougainvillea is dried because of the pink and lilac-red bracts.
Buddleia globosa (orange ball tree)	160 F 70 C	
Buxus sempervirens (common boxwood)	170 F 75 C	
Chrysanthemum haradjanii	160 F 70 C	
Cineraria maritima 'Candicans' (white diamond)	160 F 70 C	
Cornus florida var. rubra (pink dogwood)		Cornus becomes brown when dried in the microwave: dry them instead in silica gel for 3 to 4 days. The leaves can be dried at the same time.
Cornus kousa var. chinensis		" "
Cornus nutallii		" "
Corylopsis spicata (spiked winter hazel)	150 F 65 C	
Cotinus coggygria (Venetian sumach, smoke tree)	140 F 60 C	Pick the leaves in different seasons for dramatic color differences.
Epimedium (bishop's hat)	150 F 65 C	
Eucalyptus	170 F 75 C	Eucalyptus perriniana becomes olive green in the microwave. Other varieties keep their color pretty well.
Euphorbia (spurge)	150 F 65 C	

Latin Name (Common Name)	Temp.	Remarks
Euphorbia epithymoides	150 F 65 C	Dry because of the green yellow bracts.
Euphorbia myrsinites	170 F 80 C	Only dryable in the microwave. The stem leaves become olive green.
Euphorbia pulcherrima (poinsettia)	150 F 65 C	Also dry the red, pink, and white bracts.
Fagus (beech)	150 F 65 C	
Geum hybrid	150 F 65 C	
Gleditsia triacanthos (honey locust)	140 F 60 C	
Hebe 'Pagei'	160 F 70 C	
Hedera helix (English ivy)	175 F 80 C	Only dryable in the microwave. Loose leaves or branches can be preserved with glycerin (see Chapter 16).
Hydrangea petiolaris (climbing H)	160 F 70 C	Dry the leaves in different growth stages: just out of the buds, mature leaves, and the leaves turning yellow in the Fall.
Kochia scoparia	175 F 80 C	
Leycesteria formosa (Himalayan honeysuckle) leaves	150 F 65 C	The purple bracts with berries can only be dried in the microwave.
bracts	185 F 85 C	Let the silica gel cool completely prior to removing the branches.
Lupinus polyphyllus (lupine)	160 F 70 C	
Lychnis coronaria (rose campion)	150 F 65 C	
Mahonia aquifolium (Oregon holly)	170 F 75 C	Only dryable in the microwave where they become a green/brown.
Mahonia japonica (Japanese holly)	170 F 75 C	" "
Pachysandra terminalis	175 F 80 C	The leaf rosettes can only be dried in the microwave.

Latin Name (Common Name)	Temp.	Remarks
Passiflora coerulea (passionflower)	140 F 60 C	The leaves become bronze/green in the microwave; the leaf tendrils can be preserved with glycerin (see Chapter 16).
Polemonium foliosissimum	140 F 60 C	
Populus alba (white poplar)	160 F 70 C	On the underside the leaves are like white felt.
Prunus (flowering cherry)	140 F 60 C	
Prunus laurocerasus (cherry laurel)	170 F 75 C	Only dryable in the microwave.
Quercus (oak)	150 F 65 C	Dry leaves as they change colors in the Fall.
Rader machera	160 F 70 C	
Robinia pseudoacacia (black locust)	140 F 60 C	
Rosa (rose)	140 F 60 C	
Ruscus acutifolius (butcher's broom)	160 F 70 C	
Ruta graveolens (herb of grace or rue)	140 F 60 C	
Salix hastata 'Wehrhahnii' (snow pussy willow)	170 F 75 C	
Salix repens 'Rosmarinifolia' (creeping willow)	170 F 75 C	
Salix officinalis (common sage)	150 F 65 C	
Salvia sclarea (clary, sage)	150 F 65 C	Dry because of the bluish/white bracts.
Sambucus (elder)	150 F 65 C	
Santolina chamaecyparissus (lavender cotton)	170 F 75 C	

Latin Name (Common Name)	Temp.	Remarks
Saxifrage umbrosa (London pride)	175 F 80 C	Only dryable in the microwave. The leaf rosettes become olive green while the underside remains a reddish/brown.
Senecia laxifolius (senecio)	170 F 75 C	
Skimmia japonica foremanii	175 F 80 C	Only dryable in the microwave.
Smilicina racemosa (false Solomon's seal)	150 F 65 C	
Sorbus aria (whitebeam)	170 F 75 C	On the underside the leaves are like white felt.
Stachys lanata (lamb's ear)	150 F 65 C	Like grey felt.
Symphoricarpos albus (snowberry)	140 F 60 C	
Tellima grandiflora purpurea	140 F 60 C	
Tiarella (foam flower)	140 F 60 C	
Tulipa (tulip)	170 F 75 C	Only dryable in the microwave; becomes bronze/green.
Ulmus carpinifolia (Jersey elm)	150 F 65 C	Dries to a bronze/green in the microwave.
Verbascum thapsus (mullein)	150 F 65 C	Like grey felt.
Vinca major (big blue periwinkle)	175 F 80 C	Only dryable in the microwave.

CHAPTER THIRTEEN:
PERSONAL NOTES ON LEAF DRYING

Latin Name	Common Name	Silica Gel Temperature	Remarks

Latin Name	Common Name	Silica Gel Temperature	Remarks

Latin Name	Common Name	Silica Gel Temperature	Remarks

CHAPTER FOURTEEN:
DRYING LOOSE STEMS

Almost all flowers are dried with a short stem that is later wrapped with floral wire for arranging. In a loose arrangement, though, where floral wire would be a distracting eyesore, flowers can be put on a "borrowed" stem. These borrowed stems are dried in the microwave without silica gel after the leaves and flowers have been removed. Place five or six stems between a double layer of paper towels and cook for three to five minutes on the same setting you use for flowers. Check them after ten minutes of standing time and, if necessary, return them to the microwave.

CHAPTER FIFTEEN:
BERRIES AND SEED PODS

Berries

Most people have little or no success drying berries. Without a microwave it doesn't work at all, and with a microwave they usually burst.

The berries of Leycesteria formosa can, however, be dried in the microwave because their berries are hidden behind purple bracts and their battered condition doesn't show. These purple clusters are beautiful in bouquets. (See pages 33 and 34 for samples.)

I've had some success drying the small purple berries of the Callicarpa. Use setting #2 (about 150 watts) until the silica gel reaches 170° F (75° C). Five branches in about 2¼ pounds (1 kilogram) of silica gel takes about 12 to 14 minutes. After the standing time, remove the branches. You'll probably find about half the berries are cracked, but the other half is usable.

The berries of Cotoneaster "Cornubia" can be preserved using just glycerin. (See Chapter 16.)

Because berries are so very attractive in bouquets, you may have to compromise your preference for natural materials. The berries of imitation privet and elder can be separated from the clusters and wrapped together with floral wire for beautiful results.

Seed Pods

Generally, drying seed pods in the microwave is not successful. For the best results, dry by hanging them upside down, and pick them while they're still green. Lunaria biennis (honesty) is the one exception worth some experimenting. Dry the branches until the silica gel reaches 170° F (75° C). The pods become a shiny green which will gradually turn purple.

The green seed covers of Physalis alkekengi (Chinese lantern) also dry well in the microwave. First cut them in from the point four or five times, and then fold them open. Dry the green "flowers" in the microwave until the silica gel is 150° F (65° C). Watch through the blooming season for lanterns that are a vivid orange and dry some in the microwave and some by hanging. When you combine the two colors of lanterns with some imitation berries and ferns, it makes a beautiful, fairy-like bouquet.

CHAPTER SIXTEEN:
PRESERVING LARGE BRANCHES AND LEAVES

Obviously, the microwave is too small for drying large branches, but that doesn't mean they can't be a beautiful part of your bouquets. Branches and leaves treated in glycerin stay flexible for years. And when they've collected dust or dirt, just dip them in warm, soapy water and pat dry with paper towels. Most leaves will not discolor with time, although Hedera (ivy) and Mahonia (Oregon grape) discolor to a beige brown.

A good supply of preserved greenery can be used in many variations. Combine them with a small bunch of fresh flowers in the winter to make a substantial but inexpensive bouquet, or cluster a few sprigs together with some flowers and secure the stems together with floral wire to make small nosegays. Small nosegays made with dried material also make lovely keepsake corsages.

How to Use Glycerin

Only sturdy, mature leaves and branches are able to absorb glycerin. Pick the branches from August through the beginning of Fall. (Branches should be no longer than two feet [60 cm.]). With thick branches, remove the bark for about 2 inches (5 cm.) on the bottom, and make several slices at an angle in the stem to enlarge the absorption surface.

The glycerin solution is made from one part glycerin to two parts warm water. (The glycerin/water solution can be warmed in the microwave.)

floral tape

Place the branches upright in containers with about 1½ inches (4 cm.) of the glycerin solution surrounding the stems. Store the containers in a warm place. When all of the leaves are a dark color — about two to three weeks — the branches have absorbed enough glycerin. (Leathery leaves take a little longer.) Remove the branches from the solution and hang them on the clothesline to drip. Then rinse them with warm water and pat dry with paper towels. If the glycerin solution isn't too dirty, you can re-heat it and start preserving a new batch of branches.

If your branches begin to droop before they've changed color, remove them from the glycerin solution and hang the branches upside down until the glycerin is absorbed by the top branches.

The leaves of Lily of the Valley (Convallaria majalis) and Iris, along with the tendrils of Hedera (ivy), Passiflora (passionflower) and Clematis vitelba tend to droop long before they've absorbed the liquid. It's better to dip them in a glycerin bath made from one part boiling water to one part glycerin. Place the plant material in a large pan or tub and add the warm liquid until everything is just covered. (The leaves should lie next to one another.) Shift the branches every once in a while and cover the solution with a layer of aluminum foil.

Some plants are especially suited to this method and will last for years. Among them are: Acer (maple), Camellia, Choisya ternata (Mexican orange blossom), Clematis vitelba, Convallaria majalis (Lily of the Valley), Cotinus coggygria (Venetian Sumach), Fagus sylvatica (beech), Hedera (ivy), Ilex (holly), Iris, Mahonia, Passiflora (passionflower), Pieris, Prunus laurocerasus (cherry or common laurel), Quercus (oak), and Rhododendron.

The flowers of Hydrangea paniculata become beige when preserved in glycerin. Most berries become very dark, although the red berries of Cotoneaster "Cornubia" become a shade lighter.

CHAPTER SEVENTEEN: SAVING EVERYTHING FOR LATER

As you remember from Chapter 1, dried flowers have the unpleasant tendency to re-absorb moisture and wilt when exposed to damp atmospheres. If you live in an area with high humidity during the summer months, you'll need to find a safe place to store your dried flowers.

Loose flowers store perfectly well in flat boxes with tight-fitting covers. If your boxes are cardboard, place the boxes in plastic bags for added protection.

For extremely damp locales, store your flowers with a small bag or envelope of silica gel.

Dried leaves tend not to re-absorb moisture and can be saved in cardboard boxes without silica gel.

If you just can't resist the temptation to make a dried bouquet during a damp season, look through the charts in Chapter 9 for flowers that tend not to re-absorb moisture. The pink and white bracts of Cornus (dogwood) are beautiful in bouquets. For added protection against wilting, round out your bouquet with a hearty supply of moisture-resistant greenery. And, from time to time, spray your bouquets with a light mist of hairspray or shellac.

CHAPTER EIGHTEEN:
USING DRIED FLOWERS AND LEAVES

The creative possibilities with arranging dried flowers are endless, and so are the number of books and classes available to those eager to learn. Since I'm only a "Sunday dabbler" myself when it comes to flower arranging, I won't try to give design instructions in this book. What I do want to do, though, is leave you with several creative projects for the flowers you can now dry so quickly.

Many people begin making their dried bouquets in the Fall, when their gardens have finished blooming and cut flowers are becoming more expensive. If your own inventory of dried flowers and leaves is running low, consider purchasing a few stems of commercially dried flowers.

Floral and craft shops are great sources for flower arranging supplies. Some items to look for are:

Dried Flower Oasis — Hard foam that doesn't absorb water. Available in blocks, sheets, balls, wreath shapes, or can be cut to size.

Floral Wire — Available in different gauges. Used to reinforce stems, secure clustered flowers, etc.

Floral Tape — Elastic tape with a gum base used to cover unsightly wire. Available in shades of green and brown. Always store the tape in a cool place to prevent the gum base from melting.

Floral Picks — U-shaped pieces of wire used to secure flowers to a base.

Oasis Picks — Plastic green picks used to attach dried material to Oasis Foam.

Oasis Fix — Strong green gluepaste used to secure picks.

Glue Stick — Used to glue fallen petals back in place.

Wire Cutter — Used to cut floral wire.

Lazy Susan — Swiveling base for arrangements that allows the bouquet to be viewed from all sides with the flick of a wrist. Available in houseware departments.

Protective Spray — Hairspray or shellac sprayed on bouquets to help prevent moisture absorption.

The stems of most dried flowers and leaves are wrapped with floral wire to make insertion into the foam core easier and prevent breakage. If your flowers were dried with a toothpick stuck into the flower head, you have two choices. You can leave the toothpick in place and wrap it with green or brown floral tape, or you can remove the toothpick and replace it with a sturdy piece of floral wire. Push the wire through the back side of the flower head and curve the top end of the wire into a small U-shape. Then pull the curved end back through the flower until it embeds securely into the flower head.

With flowers that are very fragile or do not have strong stems — such as Hollyhock — a wire stem is added as described above. If the flower head is too hard for the wire to pierce, try heating the wire over a candle flame.

Small, delicate flowers should be grouped together in small clusters and then secured together with floral wire.

In loose arrangements, floral wire and tape can sometimes be disturbing, so dried stems are slipped over the wire stem and then secured with a very small length of thin wire.

Small, light flowers can use almost any borrowed stem. Heavier flowers, though, will need a sturdy stem such as Veronica (speedwell), which has a hollow, sturdy stem when completely dry.

Hollow stems can also be stuck into the oasis by themselves first to indicate the outline of your bouquet, with the wired flowers inserted afterwards through the hollow stems.

You can reduce the required size of your oasis by packing the bottom of your vase or Lazy Susan with wood shavings or newspaper wads. The oasis is then put on top of this layer with the top of the oasis protruding above the rim of the vase. Oasis tape then fastens the oasis to the vase's rim. A tall, thin vase can be made sturdier by adding several small, dry pebbles to the bottom.

Although the bouquets in this book were photographed in front of a sunny window to make them look their finest, your dried bouquets should never be placed in direct sunlight.

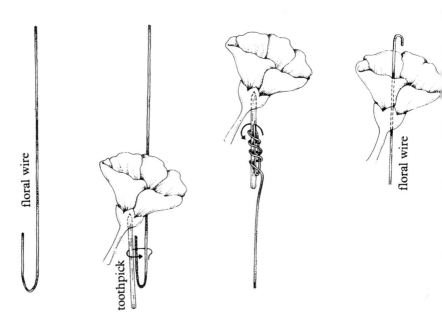

62

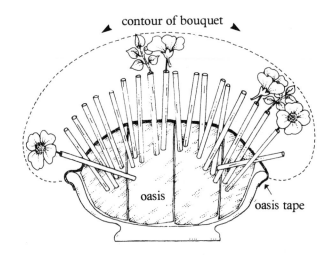

contour of bouquet

oasis

oasis tape

Bouquets Behind Glass

Because they're closed off from outside air, bouquets behind glass stay beautiful for years. A frame shop can help you find a frame with convex glass. The frame should come with a plastic back cover, but if the cover is cardboard you'll have to replace it with plastic to prevent moisture from leaking in. Bouquets can also be placed under glass in a bell jar, as shown on the back cover.

The dried material is fastened to the oasis with pins or glue. If you're using pins, stick them in through the back of the oasis to prevent them from showing. Be careful to mark the boundaries of the glass before you begin work to prevent your arrangement from being crushed when the cover is attached.

A small bag of silica gel can be hidden in the back of the bouquet for extra protection against moisture, and your picture should be hung away from direct sunlight

The framed bouquet on page 33 is eight years old and has not changed much through the years.

A bridal bouquet can be dried and framed for a very special gift. The bouquet is first taken apart, with the floral tape removed before going in the microwave. (Before taking the bouquet apart, be sure to photograph it so you'll know exactly how to put it back together.) The flowers and leaves are dried separately, species by species.

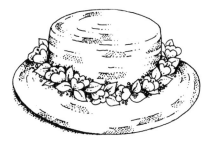

Doing More with Dried Flowers

To decorate a hat, pin or glue your dried materials onto a length of ribbon. Then attach the two ribbon ends together with pins or glue and carefully place the ribbon over the hat.

Decorated Mirror

As with the hat, attach your dried flowers and leaves first to a length of ribbon, and then glue the ribbon to the mirror's border. For a mirror without a border, attach an oasis foam border to the mirror's edge and attach the dried material with picks. The doors in your home can also be decorated using this method.

Use flowers that can stand some wear and tear such as Astrantia (masterwort), Centaurea (bachelor button), Deutzia (wedding bells), Exochorda (pearlbush), Hydrangea, Lysimachia clethroides (creeping Jenny), Myositis (forget-me-not), and Polygonum (knotweed). Dried branches of all kinds of Adiantum (maiden hair fern) and grey felt-like leaf species are also fairly strong. Less colorful but almost indestructible are branches preserved in glycerin. Artificial flowers and dried grasses can also be used.

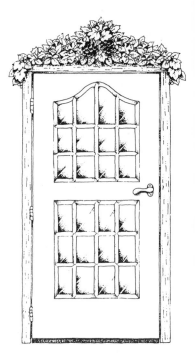

CHAPTER NINETEEN:
GARDENING IN THE WINTER

Even if there's a foot of snow on the ground outside your doorstep, the true garden lover can create a special "indoor garden" with scrap pieces of oasis foam and leftover dried materials.

To make a garden, make a base from a flat piece of foam and rest it on a flat dish or serving tray. Mountains and hills can be cut from oasis scrap and fastened to the base with toothpicks or floral picks.

Pebbles or sand make small roads and paths, and a small container of water can be pressed into the foam to make a lake.

The sides of the foam are "planted" with dried greenery, while a flower bed is made from small dried flowers. Little branches make hedges and bushes. (The dried rosette of Pachysandra becomes a palm tree; a dried Kochia branch becomes an olive tree . . . just let your imagination run wild.)

This indoor garden also makes a fun project for children, although they should be warned that an oasis base can easily break if handled roughly.

CHAPTER TWENTY:
DRIED FLOWER WREATHS

Wreaths made from dried flowers have decorated homes since Victorian times. They're quick and simple to make and are a great way to make use of leftover dried materials.

Begin making your wreath by inserting individually wired or clustered flowers onto the top of a wreath-shaped base with floral pins or picks. Bases of natural materials — such as moss, twigs, straw, or vines — are easiest to insert picks, pins, and wire into. You can purchase these bases in craft supply stores or make your own from accessible natural materials.

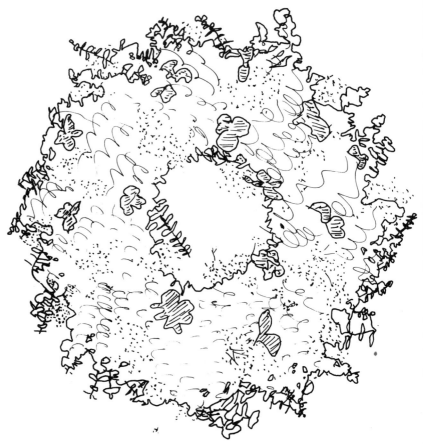

Continue placing your flowers around the top of the wreath, leaving 1 to 2 inches (5 cm.) of each flower exposed as you add each new one. Always work in one direction, turning the base as you go. When you're finished, clip any errant flowers or leaves that disrupt the symmetry of your design.

Another option is to leave part of your base exposed or to wrap the base with a wide ribbon at an angle and let it show.

Many herbs and spices can also be dried in the microwave to make beautiful, fragrant additions to any wreath. Among them are: ambrosia, artemisia, basil, bay leaves, chervil, chilies, chives, cinnamon, cloves, dill, feverfew, garlic, horehound, lamb's ear, marjoram, mint, rosemary, rue, sage, savory, thyme, wormwood, and yarrow. Experiment with cooking times the same way you did with un-listed flowers and leaves and record your results.

Other wreath materials to consider are: pine cones; small children's toys, such as wooden blocks or stuffed teddy bears; fruits, vegetables, and animals made from silk; small elements taken from Christmas tree ornaments, such as toy drummers, animals, trains, etc. These items can be attached to your wreath's base with hot glue or can be wired to the base.

ALPHABETICAL LIST OF COMMON PLANT NAMES WITH LATIN NAMES

A

Aaron's beard .... Saxifraga
Acacia .... Acacia decurrens
African marigold .... Tagetes
Avens .... Geum

B

Bachelor's button .... Centaurea montanana
Beech .... Fagus
Bergenia .... Bergenia
Black locust .... Acacia
Bridal wreath .... Spiraea vanhouttii
Butcher's broom .... Ruscus
Buttercup .... Ranunculus

C

Candytuft .... Iberis
California poppy .... Eschscholzia
Cape marigold .... Dimorphotheca
Catchfly .... Lychnis viscaria
Chamomile .... Anthemis nobilis
Chrysanthum .... Chrysanthenum carninatum
Colewort .... Crambe cordifolia
Columbine .... Aquilegia
Common box .... Buxus sempervirens
Coralbells .... Heuchera
Cow parsnip .... Heracleum
Cosmos .... Cosmea
Creeping willow .... Salix repens
Crown of thorns .... Euphorbia splendens

D

Daylily .... Hemerocallis
Dill .... Anethenum
Dogwood .... Cornus
Dusty miller .... Senecio
Dwarf goat's beard .... Astilbe chinensis pumila

E

Elderberry .... Sambucus
Elm .... Ulmus
English box .... Buxus sempervirens
Eryngium .... Eryngium
Euphorbia .... Euphorbia

F

Feverfew .... Chrysanthenum parthenium
Fleece flower .... Polygonum
Flowering quince .... Chaenometes japonica
Forget-me-not .... Myosotis
Foxglove .... Digitalis
French hydrangea .... Hydrangea macrophylla

G

Gaura .... Gaura
Golden beauty .... Bupthalmum
Goldenrod .... Solidago
Gooseneck .... Lysimachia cletroides
Greek valerian .... Polemonium caeruleum

H

Heath .... Erica
Himalayan blue poppy .... Meconopsis betonicafolia
Himalayan honeysuckle .... Leycesteria formosa
Hollyhock .... Althaea rosea
Honesty .... Lunaria biennis
Honey locust .... Gleditschia triacanthos

I

Ivy .... Hedera

J

Jacob's ladder .... Polemonium
Jew's mallow .... Kerria
Joe Pye weed .... Eupatorium purpureum

L

Lamb's tongue (or ear) .... Stachys
Larkspur .... Delphenium
Lavender .... Santolina
Lilac .... Syringa
Lupine .... Lupinus

M

Maidenhair fern .... Adiantum
Maple .... Acer
Marsh marigold .... Caltha
Masterwort .... Astrantia
Milkweed .... Asclepias tuberosa
Mock orange .... Philadelphus
Money plant .... Lunaria biennis
Mountain ash .... Sorbus aria
Mountain bluet .... Centaurea montana
Mullein .... Verbascum

O

Oak .... Quercus
Ox-eye chamomile .... Anthemis tinctoria

P

Passionflower .... Passiflora
Pearlbush .... Exochorda giraldei
Periwinkle .... Vinca
Poached egg flower .... Limnanthus douglasii
Poinsettia .... Euphorbia pulcherrima

R

Rockfoil .... Saxifrage
Rose .... Rosa
Rue .... Ruta graveolens

S

Salvia	Salvia sclarea
Santolina	Santolina
Scarlet plume spurge	Euphorbia fulgens
Scotch broom	Cytisus
Shrimp plant	Beloperene guttata
Snowball	Viburnum
Snowberry	Symphoricarpus
Speedwell	Veronica
Spurge	Euphorbia
St. John's wort	Hyperincum
Star of Bethlehem	Ornithogalum
Strawberry geranium	Saxifraga

T

Transvaal daisy	Gerbera
Tree fern	Blechnum
Tulip	Tulipa

V

Venetian sumach	Cotinus

W

Water avens	Geum rivale
Wattle	Acacia
Waxflower	Hoya
Wedding bells	Deutzia
White poplar	Populus alba
Willow	Salix
Winter rose	Helleborus
Witch hazel	Hamamelis
Wormwood	Artemisia

Y

Yarrow	Achillae